Table of Contents
Copyright Information
Introduction

Introduction

The excitement and anticipation had been building up for weeks beforehand; the promise that their parents gave that they would take them to see all the animals at the zoo on Easter Sunday if they were good, had arrived at last! Over the last two weeks, all three of them, two sisters, Susan, Evelyn, and Liam, were on their best behaviour, coming up to the Easter holidays!

The trip to the zoo in their dad's car was full of excitement, and Evelyn, Susan, and Liam kept asking their Mom and Dad about all the different animals that they would see. "How close would we get to the lions" asked Susan, and before dad could answer her, Evelyn asked mom "Will we be able to pull the monkeys tails, she said with a giggle?

Liam wanted to know all about the Kangaroos from Australia as he had watched the movies each week on television about "Skippy, the bush Kangaroo".

They arrived at the zoo car park at around 11 o'clock in the morning, and walked to the zoo gates holding hands with each other. It was a beautiful day with the birds singing and the sun was shining brightly!

After paying and going through the stiles, Liam lost sight of his family because of the hundreds of people coming and going in all directions. He thought that they must have gone ahead of him and he started to run to try to catch up, but he couldn't see them anywhere.

After running around for a long time, he sat down on a low wall which was around the flower beds. Liam was very scared and was about to cry when this small shaggy dog with long hair came sniffing around and stopped beside him and said:

"Hello little boy, my name is Fido, why are you so looking so sad?"
"My name is Liam and I've lost my family in the crowd of people, and I don't know what to do?" replied Liam.

Fido told Liam not to worry because he too was lost and had been for several weeks, but he knows all the animals in the zoo and they would surely help him find his family. "Firstly, let's go to see my friend Leo the Lion who is close by and ask him for his advice".
And so the adventure begins…

ZOO

Zoo animals help Liam who got lost!

ZOO

Seamus Shell

Fido

Fido the Dog

Picture of a Scottish terrier taken by Matthew MacKenzie, February 2003.Ogmios **at the English language Wikipedia**

"Hello, little boy, my name is Fido, what's your name, and why are you looking so sad?"
"Hello Fido, my name is Liam, and I've lost my family and I don't know what to do!"

"Don't worry" said Fido; "I'll help you find them. I know this zoo pretty well, because I'm lost too, just like you, and I've been here for over a month now."
Fido continued: "I have made plenty of friends among the animals and there is plenty of food to eat and drink.

The people, who visit, leave tons of food behind half eaten, like when they get fish and chips or hamburgers and only eat half of them. I soon sniff out where the food is and snatch it from the waste baskets. I've nearly been caught a few times by the security guards, but I always managed to escape, so far so good!"

"I've got an idea, if we visit each of the animals and ask their advice about how we can find your parents, they may be able to help us.

Firstly, let's go and see my friend 'Leo the lion' as he is the closest animal to where we are now".
"That's a good idea" replied Liam who was very excited about seeing Leo and off they went to see the big lion!

LEO

Leo the Lion

Barbary lion at the New York Zoo. Photo courtesy Nelson Robinson 1897

Fido told me that the lion's name was Leo, so when we arrived at the lion's den, Fido greeted the big lion: "Hello Leo, this is my friend Liam, who has lost his parents, and we would like to ask you what you think we should do to find them?" Leo growled with a grunt which startled Liam, but Fido reassured Liam that Leo was his friend and would not do them any harm!

"My advice would be for you to stay here with me and enjoy the sun for 3 or 4 hours, and you can rest or fall asleep if you like. No one will harm you when you're with me growled Leo". After looking at his large teeth and his sharp claws Liam believed him that while they were with him under his protection, no one no matter how big and strong they were would dare come near them.

 "Then when you wake up, continued Leo, we will both be hungry, and my zoo keeper will bring me a leg of a cow to eat and you can have some of it too. By that time, your parents should have visited the other animals, and when they visit me, they will see you and you will be together again.

Leo gave a big **Roarrrrrrrrrrr!** And they could see his teeth and his two sharp fangs when he opened his mouth. Wow, that was scary, Liam thought as he imagined being bitten by the fierce lion in front of him.

Hymm, thought Fido as he looked at Liam and said: "That's great advice that Leo has given us and we should thank him, but I think we will keep looking for your parents while there's plenty of daylight left". They both thanked Leo for his advice, and for his generous offer to share the cow's leg with them when it arrived, and wished him to have a great day!

"Imagine eating a raw cow's leg and sharing it with Leo, laughed Liam" "Yeah, it's no wonder that the lion is called the 'King of the Jungle'. "We would be lucky if he didn't eat us alive as well. I sure don't fancy staying in a lion's den with a hungry lion as fierce as Leo is" said Fido.

"He might be a little friendly right now because he's just been fed and is a bit sleepy, but later on when he gets hungry is when we would better watch out! Let's see what the Giraffe has to say" replied Fido, as he ran ahead to where his friend stretch the giraffe was feeding himself by eating the leaves off the top of the trees.

Stretch

Stretch the Giraffe

Author: Steve Garvie from Dunfermline, Fife, Scotland **8 July 2010**

"Hello Stretch, barked Fido, this is my friend Liam who has lost his family"

"Hello Liam, don't worry, I will help you to find them" said Stretch, as he knelt down on his knees. "Climb up on my back and then climb up my long neck to the top of my head and you will be able to see everyone from that height" Liam did as the giraffe told him, and when he had climbed onto his back, the giraffe stood up on his long legs and encouraged Liam to begin climbing up his neck.

As Liam climbed higher and higher up the Giraffe's neck using his legs to push up, while pulling with his arms to reach the top, where he was level with the Giraffe's eyes, he looked down from where he was and he started to feel dizzy. He was quite scared that he might fall as this was the highest he had ever climbed before. Stretch started walking around in a circle so Liam could have a better view all around.

Liam could see everywhere all over the zoo from this height, and after a quick look around, he slid down the neck of the giraffe and off his back. "I couldn't see my family as there were too many people, there must have been millions of them going in every direction.

Thanks for your help Stretch; it was nice of you to help!" Feeling excited after being up so high, Liam was glad to be safely down on the ground again and continued: "Well that was a good idea Stretch. I thought that being up so high I would be able to see my family, but looking down at all the people who were going in all directions it was so hard to pick out anybody, at least we tried even though it didn't work"

Yes that's the main thing, at least we gave it a go, Fido agreed. After thanking Stretch, Fido and Liam waved goodbye and went on to the next animal, the Gorilla.

Silvery

Silvery the Gorilla

Male Silverback Gorilla   Author: Brocken Inaglory

"Hello Silvery, barked Fido, this is my friend Liam, and we are trying to find Liam's family because he got separated from his parents and two sisters in the crowd. We wonder if you could help us in some way to try and find them"

"Hello Liam, how are you?" said Silvery. "I have a little gorilla about your age myself, and he is always getting lost. However, I only have to pound on my chest loud enough and he can hear me. It takes a lot of energy to pound my chest and call out loud, so I need to eat an orange or a bunch of bananas to give me the energy. Do you have any bananas or oranges, so I can help you much better?" "Liam replied that he was sorry, but he didn't have any fruit at all, as his parents had all the fruit with them".

"Never mind" the gorilla answered. "I'll do my best", and he started to

11

pound his chest with his huge arms while making as loud a roar as he could at the same time".

It was no good, as all that happened was that about 20 or 30 people came to see what all the commotion was about and none of them were Liam's family. Silvery seemed quite happy that his noise making had attracted a larger crowd as he and his family of gorillas liked the attention of people, firstly because it made them feel important, and secondly they knew that they would get more food as the people would throw nuts, oranges and bananas to them.

Sometimes they would be thrown food that was not good for them, food that doesn't grow on trees, like sweets, potato crisps, and other unnatural foods. They certainly wouldn't find that kind of food in the jungle. Perhaps that is why there is a sign at the entrance to the gorilla enclosure saying: Please don't feed the animals!

They thanked Silvery for trying to help as best he could and wished him a good day! It was off to the next animal now, and I wonder who it will be thought Liam.

Snoopy and Doupy

Snoopy and Doupy - the Hyenas

Spotted hyena cubs at their den. Author: GalliasM

As Liam and Fido came to a bend in the road, they could hear the sound of laughter which seemed to be coming from just around the corner. Curious to see what all this laughing was about, they walked in the direction of the noise as it got louder and louder the closer they got to it.

There were the culprits, there they were, the source of the laughter, as Liam and Fido saw two Hyenas laughing away to their hearts content. Jumping and chasing each other on the dusty ground, were Snoopy and Doupy, the laughing hyena cubs.

"Hello my friends" said Fido. "Liam and I are looking for Liam's parents and his two Sisters, Susan and Evelyn, but we can't find them. Have you guys any idea of how we can find them?"

"None at all, at all" said Snoopy, "none at all, at all", answered Doupy, "he, he, he, he, ha, ha, ha, ha" they laughed as they rolled over and over while wrestling and playing with each other and having a great time.

Fido looked at Liam, and gave a little twist of his head to indicate to Liam that they should move on, as there was no point in talking to these silly clowns. They were too young to know anything about anything thought Fido. "All they are interested in is playing and having fun; they don't realise that I asked them a serious question" said Fido.

"Yeah, just look at them rolling around in the sandy soil jumping on each other and chasing after the tail of each other" Liam remarked to Fido. "They are so funny and stupid the way that they are carrying on, ha, ha, ha", laughed Liam, forgetting for a moment that he was still lost and needed to find his parents and sisters.

"OK, enjoy the rest of the day" Fido said as he and Liam moved on to the next animal. "I hope the rest of the animals we see won't be as silly as these two" Liam said to Fido.

"Ha, ha, ha, ha" Fido laughed! "They sure are crazy critters!" he said, and off they skipped to the next animal.

Skippy

Skippy the red Kangaroo

Female Red Kangaroo   Author: Bidgee 7 December 2008

When Liam and Fido came upon the next animal, Liam was delighted to see his favourite animal, the Australian Kangaroo or Skippy as he loved to call him. He always watched "Skippy" the bush kangaroo on television every week and felt that he knew this lovely animal very well.

"Oh, here's my favourite animal!" Liam cried out! "Wait until you see him hop, he said excitedly"! Fido greeted Skippy, the red kangaroo saying: "G'day Mate" and Skippy called back: "G'day Fido, what's up?" "I'd like to introduce my friend Liam, who has lost his family in the crowd and we're trying to find them".

"No worries mate, she'll be right. I've got an idea that might work, because when I want to find another 'roo or when I need to move on to another area where there is more food, I tell my baby joey to jump into my pouch on my tummy and I hop on my two strong legs, covering a lot of ground with each bounce, to get where I want to go"

"Let Liam, climb into my pouch and I will hop around the zoo so that he can see if he can spot his family. When I bounce up Liam will be able to see a lot higher and maybe, just maybe, he will see them".

"Sounds like a good idea to me" Fido replied. "Yeah, let's give it a go" said Liam as he climbed into the pouch. This should be fun Liam thought getting a ride in the pouch or pocket that Skippy had on his tummy.

Bounce, bounce, bounce, went Skippy with Liam clinging on inside his pouch. Uh, uh, uh, coughed Liam with each bounce hop, hop, and hop, all around the zoo they went with Liam straining his eyes as hard as he could to see if there was any sign of his mom, dad, and his two sisters. Up they went and down they came with each bounce. "Whee! This is great fun" said Liam as up they bounced again and again.

When they came back to where Fido was waiting, Liam climbed out of the pouch and thanked Skippy for being so kind and helpful, even though they didn't find what they were looking for. Unfortunately he and Fido had to move on and Fido and Liam called out to their Aussie mate:

"See you later Skippy", shouted Liam, "See you Skippy" shouted Fido, and off they went. "Wow, what a ride that was" said Liam. "Did you enjoy it asked Fido"? "Yes, I did even though it was a bumpy ride" answered Liam who couldn't help laughing, ha ha-ha! "That was better than the hobby horses or the bumping cars" Liam continued.

"So what will we do now?" asked Liam to whom Fido replied: "Let's go and see my old mate Slowie the tortoise and he'll surely know what we should do. He must know a lot of things as he is very old. Guess what age he is Liam?"

Liam guessed that he was about 35 years old. "He is 112 years old and still going strong, tortoises can live to a very ripe old age" replied Fido. "In fact they can live to around 200 years of age. I've been talking with Slowie on several occasions and he filled me in on some interesting details about his companions"

"He informed me that the previous oldest tortoise was a giant Galapagos tortoise who lived in the Galapagos Island off the coast of Ecuador in South America and he was brought to Australia where he lived happily until he died aged 175 years old"

Fido continued to tell Liam more about what Slowie told him "he also said that in the Guinness book of World Records the oldest known animal ever was a tortoise from Madagascar called Tui Malila, who died in 1966 aged 189!"

"His name was Jonathan and he was brought from the Seychelles to St Helena. Jonathan was already 50 years old when he arrived in St Helena Island in 1882, so that makes him at least 176. He lives with three lady turtles on the island and he eats grass. He lives on the same island that the French Emperor Napoleon lived on in 1815 until Napoleon died in 1821".

"Jonathan's story came to light after his photograph was discovered among a collection of Boer War images taken by LA Innes who had a studio in the island's capital Jamestown"

"Wow, that's incredible" Liam said pondering on that age –"189 years old" Liam repeated as if he could hardly believe it, they both walked slowly to see Fido's friend Slowie. Liam had never seen a tortoise before and was curious to see what these long living creatures looked like.

Slowie

Slowie the Tortoise

Tortoise Original up loader was Childzy at en.wikipedia 24 September 2008

Liam was getting a bit tired, after all the jumping and bouncing around that he had gone through with Skippy the kangaroo and was looking for a seat or somewhere to sit down for a few minutes.

"Ah, let's rest for a while Fido". He said as he sat down on what looked like a rounded piece of rock, and Fido lay at his feet. As they were resting, the rock on which Liam was sitting started to move! "Hey, hey, what's happening, this rock is moving" shouted Liam, as he jumped off. Fido started laughing at Liam, and told him that what he thought was a rock, was actually a Tortoise!

Although Liam was still a bit startled, he now saw the funny side of it, and started laughing too. Fido explained that this was his old friend Slowie. "You are so funny Slowie you really scared Liam when you started moving"!

"Say Hi, to Slowie Liam" and Liam joked with Slowie how he was fooled into thinking he was a rock! Fido explained to Slowie how Liam got lost and was looking for his family. "Oh, I see, hmmm, let me think for a few minutes" replied Slowie.

After several minutes, he came out of his trance like state, opened his eyes, and said: "I know what to do, let Liam sit on my back and I will walk around all the places that the tourists visit and we will surely find your family".

All agreed, and Liam sat on the tortoise's back while he started walking. After about half an hour they had only gone about the length of 5 houses, and Fido could see that at this snail's pace or in this case, this tortoise's pace, that it would be night-time before they got anywhere. Liam told Fido that he had to go to the toilet for a pee, and that as it was quite a way; they would have to carry on without Slowie's help.

Liam looked at Fido and caught him giving him a wink! He understood that they were getting nowhere fast, or in this case, they were getting nowhere slow! After thanking Slowie for his great effort in helping them, they set off to find the toilet, and then to seek help from another animal.

As they were walking along Liam asked Fido: "If Slowie was 112 years old, that's probably why he moves so slow, don't you think Fido? "No, I don't think so Liam replied Fido, because all tortoises move as slow as he does, that's just the way they are. They behave as if they have all the time in the world to do something and to get to wherever they're going. That's probably why they live so long because they take forever to do anything and they need forever to do it. Ha, ha, ha, ha, laughed Fido.

Ha, ha, ha, ha, laughed Liam, "you are such fun Fido!"

Spotty

Spotty the Cheetah

Author: James Temple.

The sun was shining strongly now as Liam and Fido came out of the toilets block, and Fido asked Liam if he would like an ice-cream. "I'd love one, but I don't have any money" said Liam.
"That's ok, I have some buried in a secret place. I found some money that someone lost and buried it with my bones, so let's go and dig it up and we'll be able to get an ice-cream. I wanted to give it back to whoever lost it but I didn't know where they were. So as it's only a few dollars, they shouldn't miss it too much, reasoned Fido.

"What would you like to have Liam; you can have 'rum & raisin', Chocolate malt, butter-scotch, or vanilla with chocolate topping"? "I'll have the rum and raisin, I love raisins, said Liam. Fido settled for vanilla with chocolate topping, and they sat down on the grass while eating in silence.

Liam was thinking about all the animals that they had seen and that tried to help them. "Weren't the two hyenas, silly billy's Liam said at last"?

"Ha, ha, ha, laughed Fido, they sure were, and what about Slowie the tortoise, wasn't he slow!" "Maybe that's why they call him Slow-ie", Liam said, with a giggle, he, he, he!

"We better get a move on Fido, as it will be dark in a few hours"
"You're right, let's go to the next animal" Fido said.
"We'll have to speed things up after all the time we spent with Slowie, so let's pay a visit to my fast friend Spotty, the Cheetah". Liam agreed, and off they went.

"Spotty, it's me Fido, what's up? I have a friend with me to-day, his name is Liam, and he has lost his family in the crowds, can you give us some advice what to do? We've just come from Slowie's place and he was so slow that we wasted a whole half an hour and got nowhere"

Spotty replied: "Liam, climb onto my back and I'll make up for the time you lost, as I can run at over 70 miles or 112 kilometres an hour, not like the 2 miles or about 3 kilometres that Slowie goes at. At the speed I go at we will go all around the zoo in a jiffy"

 Liam climbed onto Spotty's back while Fido waited where he was, and they took off like a rocket, with Liam hanging onto Spotty's neck. Round and round they went and Liam spotted Fido at least 5 times as they passed him each time. Fido was sitting down waiting for them to finish their gallivanting around the zoo. Each time that Spotty and Liam whizzed past Fido, Liam would shout out "Fidoooooooooooo" as they disappeared into the distance away from Fido.

Fido had had enough of this waiting around while they seemed to be having all the fun and he jumped out in front of them the next time they came around waving his hands to stop them from going around the zoo a sixth time.

"Whew! That was so fast, that everything was a blur and I could hardly see anybody" said Liam

Fido and Liam thanked their fast friend for his effort and Spotty replied: "Sorry for not being able to see your family Liam, maybe I was going too fast" he panted, almost out of breath after carrying Liam so many times around the zoo. "Don't worry Spotty, you did a great job and we are very thankful!" said Liam, and off they went to see another zoo animal.

Freddie

Freddie the Fox

Author: Rob Lee, from Evergreen, Co, USA, 12 February 2006.
www.flickr.com/photos/roblee/11655198/in/set-1357853/

Freddie the fox was another friend that Fido had made since he too was lost in the zoo. Over the 4 or 5 weeks that Fido spent chatting with the animals, he never met anyone who was as cunning as Freddie the Fox. "Hey Freddie, how are you, Liam and myself are trying to find Liam's lost family, and we wondered if you might have some ideas how we can find them?"

"Is Liam your friend Fido"? asked Freddie.

"Yes, we met here at the zoo, and Liam told me how he got lost in the crowd of people" "Well don't worry; any friend of yours is a friend of mine." said Freddie "Nice to meet you Liam", Freddie continued, "let's see now, hmmm, I know, why don't you two help me to get into the chicken coup by distracting the chickens.

"I will give you some corn meal so you and Fido can feed the chickens from the left hand side of the chicken coop and that will allow me to sneak in on the right hand side without been seen. That way I can sneak in and grab a chicken by surprise, and after eating the chicken, I'll be able to concentrate on finding your family, without thinking of how hungry I am?" That's a good idea don't you think"? asked Freddie.

Fido and Liam whispered to each other as they discussed what Freddie had said and they came to the conclusion that that was not a good idea.

Firstly, they didn't want to do anything wrong and tricking the poor chickens by feeding them on the left side of the chicken coop so that Freddie the fox could sneak in and kill one of them was not a good thing to do!

Secondly, the security guards would surely be alerted when the chickens started to scream and make a terrible commotion when being attacked by Freddie. When they arrived to see what all the fuss was about Fido and Liam would be caught.

Thirdly, Fido had made friends with the chickens. His best chicken friend was called 'Pecky', and he wouldn't want to see Freddie eating him.

Fido replied: "Thanks all the same Freddie, but we don't have time for that" not wanting to offend the wily fox. "It won't be long now until its feeding time and you won't be so hungry then that you want to kill the chickens. We'll see you the next time we come to the zoo. It was nice seeing you!" "Yes it was nice seeing you, bye, said Liam and off they went on their quest to find the answer they were looking for.

On the way out from visiting Freddie, Fido and Liam continued to talk about the scheme that Freddie had hatched out in order to get a chicken for himself.

"Apart from everything else, if we did help Freddie I would have been in trouble with my parents when they found out about our being involved in the chicken and fox plan. We were lucky we didn't fall into Freddie's trap!" replied Liam.

"We sure were, agreed Fido!"

Quasmo

Quasmo the Monkey

Author: Chris huh. 17 July 2007 Crab-eating macaque (Macaca fascicularis) in Lopburi, Thailand.

Fido's next friend was a monkey called Quasmo, who looked very intelligent and maybe he could come up with the answer we were seeking. There were other monkeys in the enclosure and they were all doing different things: some were eating nuts, others were playing catch me if you can as they swung by their tails and arms from the branches of the trees, and a couple of monkeys were pulling each other's tails for fun. One of the monkeys was enjoying a banana quietly in a corner not wanting to attract too much attention from the others as he peeled the skin of the banana.

Fido called out to Quasmo who was busy trying to figure out how the ball he was playing with, rolled. Dropping the ball, he went over to his friend Fido who introduced Liam to him and told him the story of how Liam was lost, and would be so happy if he could help them find his family.

Distracted by another screeching monkey who pulled his tail, Quasmo couldn't seem to concentrate long enough to find the answer, and now the ball came rolling down the sloping ground to where he was trying to talk to Fido. Another monkey had rolled it and now that caught Quasmo's attention.

Fido told Liam quietly that these monkeys were scatter brains, and they might as well move on because it didn't look like Quasmo would be much of a help. "Nice seeing you Quasmo", Fido said, and Liam waved goodbye.

When they were far enough away so Quasmo couldn't hear them talking, Fido confided to Liam that "Those monkeys are almost as silly as Snoopy and Doupy the hyenas, don't you think? Liam had to agree. "They are scatter brains all right, but they are so funny"! Ha ha ha!

There was always a good crowd around the monkey enclosure and people loved to stare dreamily on the monkeys as they went about their daily business. Perhaps it is because they resemble us humans so much that makes them so attractive.

We humans love to compare them with ourselves as if that's how we used to be millions of years ago. But Liam remembers his Mom telling him that there is no connection between monkeys and human beings. Anyway, that's another story and soon they came to where the Squirrels hung out.

Nuts

Nuts the Squirrel (in the middle)

Author: Chicoutimi **(montage)**

1. Karakal
2. AndiW
3. National Park Service
4. en:User:Markus Krötzsch
5. The Lilac Breasted Roller
6. Nico Conradie from Centurion, South Africa
7. Hans Hillewaert
8. Sylvouille
9. National Park Service

"Hey Nuts" Fido called out, and number 5, the squirrel in the middle of the nine squirrels came running over. This is my new friend Liam, and he lost his family, can you suggest anything that could help us find them?"

Still chewing on a nut that he had put in his mouth before he was called, Nuts hesitated before answering, as he finished chewing and swallowed the nut. "Nice to meet you Fido and Liam" he said, as he put on his thinking cap.

"Let me think, hmmm, yes, that's it" he said, as he thought out loud. "Sometimes for a change I like to have some peanuts and hazelnuts, but the zoo keepers only give us squirrels, walnuts and Brazil nuts along with other stuff to eat"

"So, I've been hoarding lots of walnuts and Brazil nuts and I can give some to you so you can swap them at the ice-cream shop across the road for some hazelnuts and peanuts. Tom, the man who owns the ice-cream shop knows me, and if you do that swap for me, I will be able to give each of you a sample of all four nuts, so that you will have the energy to keep going on your search for the family you're trying to find. OK?"

Fido and Liam agreed, and took Nuts up on his offer. They exchanged the walnuts and Brazil nuts for peanuts and hazelnuts, with Tom the ice-cream man, who when he knew who they were for, told Liam and Fido to: "tell Nuts that he was asking for him".

"Sure, and thanks for the nuts!" said Fido. After giving the peanuts and hazelnuts to 'Nuts the squirrel', who in turn gave a few of the four nuts he now had to Liam and Fido. These were: peanuts, hazelnuts, walnuts, and Brazil nuts.

Stocked up with loads of nuts Liam and Fido were on their way again after thanking 'Nuts the squirrel' for the nuts. Now they had enough nuts to give them energy to carry on.

As Liam and Fido were walking and talking, between crunching nuts between their teeth, on their way to the next animal, Fido suggested that they try something different this time. Let's go to the Aviary where all the birds lived and ask my friend Olli the Owl for help. "I've heard stories about how wise the owl is, and he is sure to give us some good advice! What do you think Liam?"

"Yeah, let's go to see the Owl" replied Liam.

Olli

Olli the Owl

Athene_noctua_ (portrait).jpg: Trebol-a derivative work: Stemonitis (talk)

The Aviary was a huge cage like area where all the colourful birds from all around the world were kept. The cages were so big that there were trees growing inside it, and the birds could fly around without any problem. There were birds from South America where the mighty Amazon River flows that had beautiful colours of red, yellow, purple, green and blue feathers.

Liam remembered seeing one on the 'zoo sign' earlier, just before he met Fido at the start, but these ones were much larger. As they passed the parrots one of them said "Hello" in a squeaky voice and Liam said "Hello" back to him.

As they continued, the noise of the birds was quiet loud, as dozens of birds of all different species were singing and calling out to each other. Where is Olli the Owl, Liam thought to himself, as they made their way deeper and deeper into the Aviary? The farther they went the quieter it got, until near the end of the aviary they saw where Olli lived.

There he was sitting on a rock fast asleep. His eyes were closed, and he was as still as a post. What a shame that he was asleep, but owl's sleep during the day and hunt at night-time. When the sun went down and it got dark, Olli's eyes opened wide, with the pupil's in his eyes getting larger the darker it got.

This allowed Olli to see in the dark as his eyes could pick up every bit of moonlight to help him see at night-time. He was able to swoop down and catch a mouse even when it was pitch black in the middle of the night. Fido knew that it was late in the day, and Olli would soon be waking up. He also knew that it would be feeding time at the zoo soon and when all the animals had been fed, the zoo would close soon after.

"We have only a short time left Liam, so I think that we'll have to wake Olli up. I don't like doing this but we've got no other choice, time is running out". Fido continued:

"Liam, go and collect a handful of small pebbles and some soft lumps of clay and throw it at Olli in order to wake him up". Sure enough, after only the first throw of sandy soil, which had a few tiny pebbles in it about the size of raisins, Olli woke up."

"Wha! what? whau!", Olli blurted out as he was a bit startled at being woken up so suddenly! His big round eyes looked straight at Liam, as if challenging him to throw some more stuff at him, now that he's awake! **"What's going on, what's happening, why are you throwing rocks and stuff at me, what's the meaning of this, why did you wake me up?"** Olli asked in a rather loud voice.

 Yes, Liam and Fido could tell that he wasn't very happy about it, and they both quickly apologised for waking him up!

"We're very sorry Olli, we only threw tiny pebbles and a bit of sand at you we didn't mean to wake you up on purpose, but my friend Liam is getting very worried now that he can't find his family, he's lost, and we've asked nearly all the animals for help, but it's been no use. They all tried to help, but now it's getting late and you are our last hope of finding them.

31

We've heard that Owls are very wise so that is why we came to see you. What should we do?"

Olli stared at them with his big brown eyes and agreed with them that he was a wise Owl, and told them to: **"go and tell their story to a person in uniform, or to a policeman or woman, and they would know what to do.** If you don't see a **uniformed person** soon, make your way back to the entrance gate where you came in, it's the first turning on your left and straight ahead, you can't miss it" he assured them!"

"Tell the person who sells the tickets, or someone in **uniform** your story and they will find your parents and sisters for you. I'm sure that they must be very worried about you as well!" "Luckily there is only one way out of the zoo, and that's through the gates where you came in.

The gates are entrance gates and exit gates. The only difference is you only pay coming in to the zoo. They don't charge you for going out of the exit gates, Olli said with a smile, as if to show off his great wisdom and knowledge and of course his sense of humour.

Fido and Liam thanked Olli the owl very much, as this was the best advice that they had received all day! No wonder they call you **"The Wise Owl"** said Fido. "I'm really very sorry for waking you up and thank you very much Olli and I hope you have a great night!"

They had only gone a few blocks when they saw a police woman and a police man patrolling the ground of the zoo. The two police officers talked on their radio walkie talkies, and took them to the waiting room where Liam's family were waiting impatiently for him.

"Oh, my baby, my baby, where have you been?" cried Liam's Mother, "we looked everywhere for you, we thought that you might have got eaten by a Lion", she laughed, while wiping away the tears of joy from her face.

Liam's Dad smiled at him, and his sisters bombarded him with questions, asking him: "where have you been, what did you do, who did you meet, who is this dog that keeps following you?" Before Liam could answer, his Dad said:
"There will be plenty of time later for all those questions, but right now it is after 3 o'clock so if we are to see any animals *at all, at all* we better get going, as the zoo closes at 5.30 pm. We've got just over two hours to see

everything". Liam and Fido were laughing away and when Liam's Dad asked him: "what's so funny?" Liam replied that:

"There are two hyenas down that pathway that speak just like you Dad, they said none *'at all, at all'* they must be Irish hyenas", ha, ha, ha, ha, laughed Liam who was in a joking and happy mood now that he was with his family!"

After several happy hours of looking at the animals it was time to go home. "Let's go to the car-park and go home, we've had enough for to-day" Liam's Dad said.

They all held hands, with Liam's Mother keeping a tight grip on him. They had only gone through the exit gates and walked a short distance when Liam realised that Fido was not with them. He had forgotten about him in all the excitement.

"Where's Fido, where's Fido?" he repeated as he pleaded with his Dad to let him get Fido who was inside the gates and had not followed them outside as they went through the zoo gates. "He saved me Dad, he helped me, he took me to all his animal friends asking them for help, and I would still be lost without him. He's lost too, he has nobody to take care of him, please Mom, Dad please, let's take Fido too!"

Seeing the tears in his Son's eyes, and how much he wanted Fido, his Dad said to his wife (Liam's Mother)" "Stay right where you are, don't move, we'll be back in a minute".

As Liam and his Dad approached the gates, they saw Fido walking away with his head low and looking very sad. Fido, Fido, Liam called out, come with us, we want you to be part of our family. We don't have a dog, and we were going to get one anyway. Won't you come with us, please Fido; we'd love to have you!"

Fido agreed, wagging his tail furiously as he ran back to Liam! "Oh, we're going to have such a good time together" Liam told Fido and continued to tell about all the wonderful things that they would do like: going for long walks in the countryside together, where Fido could run around chasing rabbits and birds.

"We will play in our own backyard and you will be able to chase after the ball and fetch the stick that I'll throw for you" Liam continued to tell Fido. Susan and Evelyn also were excited to tell Fido about the things they could do together as well, and Fido was so happy to be another member of the family.

When the family first arrived at the zoo, there were 5 of them, Mom, Dad, Susan, Evelyn, and Liam. Now there was Fido as well, who wasn't lost any more. He had found a lovely family to live with.

Liam was no longer lost as well, and he had gained a new friend and companion in Fido. Susan, Evelyn, Liam's Mom and Dad were all very happy to have Fido in their family and took turns at patting him. So 5 came to the zoo and 6 went home, and they all lived happily ever after!

amazon.com/ZOO-ebook/dp/B007ZXQDV0/ref=sr_1_1?s=digital-text&ie=UTF8&qid=1336625306&sr=1-1

Other books by Seamus Shell:

EXTINCT!

Volume 1

http://www.amazon.com/EXTINCT!-ebook/dp/B007ZKMB5U/ref=sr_1_1?s=digital-text&ie=UTF8&qid=1336161802&sr=1-1

EXTINCT!

Volume 2

http://www.amazon.com/EXTINCT!-ebook/dp/B0080K8G9E/ref=sr_1_cc_1?s=aps&ie=UTF8&qid=13366 22558&sr=1-1-catcorr

Poems

By

Seamus Shell